Hippies, Hindus and Rock & Roll

by

Bob Larson

© Copyright 1969
Bob Larson
McCook, Nebraska

Copyright © 2025 Ultimatum Editions.
All rights reserved.

This book or any portion thereof may not be reproduced or used in any manner whatsoever without the express written permission of the publisher. The content of this book shall not be deemed to reflect the opinion or expression of the publisher or editor.

ISBN: 978-2-925611-11-0
Printed in the USA.

TABLE OF CONTENTS

FOREWORD

Half a decade ago, Bob Larson's star was rising fast as a well-known singer, composer, guitarist and disc-jockey. Today the entertainer's promising career has been eclipsed by a brighter, more fruitful enterprise whose returns are more abundant and whose rewards are eternal. What made the difference?

It was not a new lease on life for entertainer Bob Larson, but rather a lease on a New Life following the day in 1963 when he acknowledged Jesus Christ as Saviour and Lord.

Today Mr. Larson is one of the most promising young writers of religious literature. His first two books, **Rock & Roll: The Devil's Diversion,** and **Cursed Shalt Thou Be in the Cities,** have enjoyed spectacular world-wide distribution. These books analyze the effects of current events on the lives of America's youth.

The author is well qualified to speak to his contemporaries. His performances have taken him from recording studios to national television performances—including an appearance in Atlantic City's huge Convention Hall.

In 1963, as the result of a meeting with popular Country and Western entertainer, T. Texas Tyler, Mr. Larson recognized his need of salvation and took the step of faith that led to eternal life in Christ. One year later he left pre-medical studies at a large Midwestern university. His decision to enter the evangelistic ministry followed a Providential meeting with the Rev.

David Wilkerson, author of the book, **The Cross and the Switchblade,** and founder-director of Teen Challenge ministries.

In 1968, Mr. Larson signed a contract to travel as a professional lecturer on behalf of a nationally recognized agency providing assembly programs for public schools. In addition to his lecturing tours and evangelistic crusades, Larson continues to write and publish gospel songs. His record albums are popular for vocal features as well as thrilling guitar renditions.

Whichever facet of ministry he engages in—music or preaching—the young evangelist never compromises his contention that a personal relationship with Jesus Christ is the only deliverance from the grinding frustrations of modern youth.

Hippies, Hindus and Rock & Roll puts reason into the perplexing problems of today and calls for solutions that may surprise you.

The Publishers

BOB LARSON

CHAPTER ONE

A History of

The Hippie Heresy

Who is a hippie?

The obvious answer might be a person with long hair, dirty clothing, drugs and psychedelic patterns of speech and action—but the real characteristics lie much deeper.

What does a hippie believe?

Despite their growing numbers and their enormous publicity, few people understand what the "flower children" believe or what their presence portends for Western civilization. Unfortunately, they are often compared incorrectly with New Testament Christians and referred to as "gentle people" who are intellectually sincere in what they say.

The hippie movement is heralded as a modern phenomenon but its philosophical origin and attitudes are anything but new. They call Christ a "groovy cat," but this was the pompous opinion of Diogenes, a Greek Cynic philosopher of the fifth century. They advocate "dropping out," of organized society, but this was the cry of Buddha in the sixth century. Like Ghandi, they advocate nonviolent resistance and align themselves with Aldous Huxley in their praise of hallucinogenic drugs.

Their mode of retirement from community living is patterned after that of nineteenth century poet Henry David Thoreau and his retreat at Walden Pond. Their bohemian ways are not unlike those of Edgar Allen Poe, the severe poet who originated mysterious fiction bordering on the macabre. All through the centuries, the hippie hero has gained a following among his contemporaries.

At the turn of the century in America, bohemian enclaves were springing up in many American cities—the biggest center locating in New York's Greenwich Village. But the Civil War suddenly cut short these free-living societies and the two world wars and an economic depression that followed killed enthusiasm for this kind of life which a society on the rise to affluency could not tolerate.

The depression passed and the wars came to an end, and with it came an emphasis on material conformity. Parents wanted to spare their children the agony of insecurity they had known. The advertising industry instilled in children the importance of material goods. Adults, haunted by the hardships of bread lines, were thankful to be part of an economically productive nation on the move.

Then came the dawn of the nuclear age and the guilty feelings of awesome devastation which the atom bomb had accomplished. The tensions of nuclear holocaust began to create a generation of pessimistic youth. The horror of the atomic trigger lurked in their imaginations and they grew skeptical and fearful of the future. Annihilation seemed to be inevitable.

This tension began to draw out of society disillusioned beatniks without a star to reach for. They were a disgruntled lot, and few people paid much attention to them. Adults assured themselves that most teenagers were still primarily interested in Friday night's football game and Saturday's date.

But the movement persisted until the hippie cult sprang into notoriety in 1966. They borrowed a sprinkling of ideas and behavior from the beatniks but they were distinct from them. They called themselves the "Now Generation," rebelling against the disciples of education, sickened by the hypocritical insincerity of the mass media, tired of life without a goal.

Like flowers after spring rains, hippie cultures began springing up around the world. At first they had no formal communication, but gradually they developed an underground network to gather and disseminate information. The separate cultures were found to be surprisingly alike. They seemed to have a common origin which I believe lies in the mind and heart of Satan. Their conduct and propaganda manifest themselves as the spirit of the Antichrist.

The "now" people began openly to subvert the order of Western societies through the sheer and innocent-sounding method of "flower power." They preached against the state values of the West as a contradiction in contemporary life. They sought total withdrawal from the "rat-race" to begin a quest for individual identity. The secular press glorified them; teenagers ran away from home to join them; members found strength and courage for their uninhibited indulgences in the company of those of like frustrations.

The thread which has knitted all factions of the hippie movement together is the drug experience. Hippies look upon the psychedelic "trip" as the avenue to mysticism. High on Lysergic Acid Diethylamide (LSD) they sit and chant, "Let's all be Jesus till it starts to hurt!"

Some time ago I picked up a hippie underground newspaper in the Yorkville section of Toronto, Canada. Included was a feature article advising the reader how to take an LSD trip. The author stated:

> "Arrange to take the acid in a pleasant place with someone else with you at the time. Be what you are, what the moment dictates, experiencing yourself and the world without your intellect. A full course of trips properly taken will make you a better and freer, more real and loving human being. The first phase should take place in a tranquil environment. The second phase starts with slow walks. Eventually you can take small excursions and finally take acid and go about your normal business."

Tragically misinformed, some Christian believers at first looked upon hippies as promising prospects through whom the Church could present the claims of Jesus Christ. Clergymen mistakenly proclaimed that hippies were searching for truth and meaning and needed only to be guided. Wasn't their talk about love? Weren't they seeking an opportunity to share the love of God with others?

On the contrary, the hippies claimed to have found meaning for existence through conscious expanding drugs. And although they sang of love in chants and groans, they knew nothing of love's commitment and concern and duty toward one's neighbor. They ignored the responsibility of love and dwelt upon their quest for uninhibited physical gratification.

Christians who applauded the religious interest of hippies failed to understand what the search was all about. The hippie was not seeking the one true God revealed in Jesus Christ through the Scriptures; they were searching instead for an impersonal, pantheistic force that would wink at their corruptness. Their common denominator of humanism could not be reconciled with the Biblical view of man's depravity after the Fall and his need of salvation. Too late, many ministers began to see that hippie non-conformity with, and rejection of, the world was hardly the same as that high spiritual quest advocated by the Apostle Paul.

Libraries and bookstands are filled with periodicals analyzing and describing the hippie movement. It is not my purpose merely to re-state what these journals say. I refer to the over-view of the phenomenon which can be described as a kind of primitivistic sect of uncertain size, loosely organized, devoted to a life of orgiastic pleasure with no interest whatever in an orderly society.

In the second century an analagous group of people organized themselves under the title of "Adamites." They were convinced that in becoming Christians they had been restored to the sinless purity of the Garden of Eden before the Fall. Their teachings, according to the August 8, 1967 issue of **National Review,** were (1) A sense of primal innocence resulting in the practice of nudity. (2) Rejection of all laws that restricted them, (3) Pacifism, (4) Sexual freedom with no guilt or shame, (5) The community ownership of goods, and (6) A cult of love. The Adamites conducted "live-ins" in parks and gardens to imitate Eden before the disobedience of the first human beings. The similarity between the modern hippie movement and that of the Adamites is obvious: both are a heretical sect within Christianized civilizations.

Initially, a tolerant society was fascinated by the hippies. Fashion trends, art motifs and advertisements exploited them. In one sense, the hippies were having a love affair with the society they professed to disdain. But soon the idealism of the novelty wore off and pragmatism took over. Racketeers muscled in on the marijuana trade. Love turned to hate, and even some hippies themselves were shocked to discover that their tribal society had not produced Utopia but rape and murder and disease. LSD was found to cause chromosome damage. Dangerous drugs such as Methadrine (speed) began to scare their users. The hippie diet of sweets, sleepless nights and indiscriminate sex invited self destruction.

In the fall of 1967 the situation had gone too far even for the extremists. The hippies of San Francisco staged a mock funeral. The death of the hippie movement was heralded with dirges and a coffin. The flower children even sought to discard the name "hippie," in favor of such labels as "Free-men," or "Freebies." The exploitation of tourists, television and the press had done their damage.

Had the end of the hippie movement finally come? Hardly. After a brief transitional period during which its image was modified, "love" has been replaced by loneliness, fear and sporadic brutality. Militancy has seeped into their attitudes, as talk of "flower power" has been replaced by armed violence.

With the coming of the yippies (a term derived from the Youth International Party) during tense political struggles, the hippie movement has gained new life through political protest. Like the hippies, yippies made their debut in San Francisco. They chose to be announced by a "strip-in." In the spring of 1968, at least fifty of them sat naked in Golden Gate Park. Several months later they celebrated a festival in Sultan, north of Seattle, Washington. An abundance of rock bands were there, including the ensembles of "Country Joe and the Fish," the "Cleanliness and Godliness Skiffel Band," "Eruminour Bandersnatch," "Mother Tucker's Yellow Duck," and "Dr. Humbead's New Tranquility String Band." The party lasted three days and three nights.

The September 13, 1968 issue of **Time** reported the proceedings in detail:: "With the morning came

13

a 'Sun Dance," the magazine stated. "The musicians played drums, chimes, tom-toms—anything at all, while the audience hopped around chanting, 'Sun! Sun! Sun! Sun . . . !' Many of the youngsters were already lighter than air on pot."

While the hippies were admittedly non-political, the yippies became actively involved in political pursuits, particularly those of the New Left and other communist causes. Ed Sanders, a leader of the "Fugs" (an obscene, underground rock group), estimates that yippies have at least 250,000 followers.

Aligned squarely with the policies of Moscow and Peking, the hippies' and the yippies' movements roll on. Satan's shock troopers have done their job well, but they could not have accomplished it without the savage, pounding beat of rock and roll.

CHAPTER TWO

East Meets West

At The Hindu Altar

Rock and roll music, more than any other single factor, gave the hippie movement popularity. Amplified by the voice of mass communications networks and boosted by the long fingers of television, the fascination of this new phenomenon seized the attention of youth and laid a base for their rebellion.

Until 1967, the idiosyncrasies of the hippies were largely ignored or considered inconsequential. Then in 1967, well known rock entertainers began to adopt the hippie philosophy. It began cropping out in their songs. Early that year the Beatles cut a release titled, "All We Need Is Love." They were singing, of course, about humanistic, universal love. Later that year the Rolling Stones added their endorsement by recording a song with the lyrical content consisting of nothing more than the declaration, "We Love You" monotonously repeated over and over and over again.

Popular rock musicians and singers also adopted the hippies' style of living. **Time** recognized the

Beatles, for example, as the "major taste-makers in hippiedom." **Look's** August 22, 1967 edition analyzed the essence of rock music in this way: "Rock music —referred to as 'love-rock' or 'acid-rock'—is a vital ingredient in their whole way of life. In its ideal form—fast and almost too loud for the normal ear to withstand—it blanks the mind, stuns the senses, and forcibly reaches out and commands all the nerve fibers and viscera of the body to the extent that you find yourself leaping and twitching to the contagious drum rhythm with unconscious abandon."

San Francisco's Haight-Ashbury district became a Mecca for hippies. Many rock groups began to make their headquarters there. Scott MacKenzie recorded "San Francisco"—a song about Haight that became the number one tune in the nation during the summer of 1967. MacKenzie's tune suggested: "If you're going to San Francisco, be sure to wear some flowers in your hair; In the streets of San Franciso, gentle people with flowers in their hair . . . . "

Hippies recognized that rock and roll music represented a medium with which they could indoctrinate the general public. Thanks to the mass communications media, they foisted their viewpoint on the nation far beyond the actual influence of their proportionate numbers. They deliberately organized rock groups to extol the virtues of drugs and "the beautiful life of the flower children."Rock bands have since assimilated the folkways of the hippie community to such an extent that today most of the top rock and roll entertainers are either hippies themselves or are very sympathetic toward the hippie concept of living.

From the beginning of their movement, hippies have searched for a religious framework within which to express their ideas. The traumatic experience of the psychedelic introspection through acid laid the groundwork for an interest in mysticism and meditation by turning people inward. Scientific and technological advancements denied Western man the comfort and assurance of spiritual under-pinings. Voices began crying, "God is dead!" and philosophers announced that the human race had arrived at the post-Christian era.

This could not continue long. Man has a God-created hunger for something that transcends the level of human knowledge and experience. So, youth had only one place left to turn: the metaphysics of the East.

By the thousands, American youth looked longingly to spiritual disciplines of Eastern mystics as they searched for insight into their own lives. Led by the rock prophets, they sought to replace marijuana with mantras and acid with asceticism. They began to explore the inner depths of their own minds and spirits.

In an exclusive interview with editors of **Life,** published on page 75 of the magazine's Christmas Day issue, 1967, Arnold Toynbee described the situation. The eminent historian said, "The West in the last few centuries has deliberately turned away from the spiritual sense. We have come to conquests of a material sense. But we are poor spiritually."

But why has Hinduism, the cult of millions in the East, become the focal point of interest for hippies and for American youth in general? Philosopher Alan Watts assesses the appeal of Hinduism in his book, **This Is It.** He writes, "The Hebrew-Christian universe is one in which moral urgency, the anxiety to be right, penetrates everything. To be wrong, therefore, arouses a metaphysical anxiety and a sense of guilt. The appeal of Eastern philosophy, is that it unveils behind the urgent realty of good and evil, a vast region of oneself about which there need be no guilt or recrimination."

The appeal of Hinduism has passed far beyond the stage of a mere fad. Many of today's idolized youth leaders are now outspoken converts to Hinduism. One such convert is the admitted homosexual poet Allen Ginsberg. While I was enrolled at the University of Nebraska he came for a speaking engagement. He arrived arm in arm with his homosexual traveling companion, a long-haired hippie named Peter. Ginsberg's recitation of his poetry was little more than a sensationalized ejaculation of four-letter words. Obscenity is his only real claim to notoriety, yet this man wields great influence among the hippies.

Ginsberg and Peter traveled to India on a freighter some time ago and both were later converted to Hinduism. The poet was also one of the organizers of the anarchy-bent revolutionaries who had a much-publicized confrontation with the Chicago police during the Democratic National Convention in 1968. Before staging the demonstration at the Hilton Hotel, Ginsberg gathered his youthful followers together on the beach near Grant's Park for a meditation session. He cheered the hippies on by chanting the

Hindu charm word, "Om" (an utterance supposed to be the symbolic expression of the Impersonal, Omnipresent Godhead) believing that its supernatural powers would render the police helpless. (More recently, the trespassing hippies who in May of 1969 took over "People's Park' in Berkeley, California resorted to Oriental religious practices to defend their actions. The night before their eviction about 150 of them gathered around a fire pit and chanted Buddhist prayers.)

Not a few evangelical Bible scholars today are teaching that the religion of the last days before the return of Christ will be an association of institutionalized Roman Catholicism and apostate Protestantism. I do not share this conviction. Present trends indicate to me that both apostate Protestanism and institutionalized Roman Catholicism will form a religious coalition greatly influenced by the religious concepts of the Orient.

A case in point is a recent ordination service at St. Mark's Episcopal Church in Berkeley, California. **Time** reporters covered the service and gave this report on page 73 of its April 22, 1968 edition: "Instead of the traditional garb, the moustached man (the hippie to be ordained) wore a psychedelic chausuble. In the background, a rock band played. He had been operating a free church that ministered to hippies in Berkeley. The church was decked out with gas-filled balloons and banners. The sermon was entitled, "God Is Doing His Thing."

George Harrison of the Beatles is responsible for much of the rising interest in Hinduism. Some time ago in a press interview, he made his religious beliefs quite plain. "Through Christianity," he said, "how I was taught it, they told me to believe in Jesus and in God and all that. They didn't actually show me any way of experiencing God or Jesus. I kicked the concept of a 'man in the sky' a long time ago. Jesus was a divine incarnation like Buddha and Krishna ...."

In 1965 Harrison became interested in Oriental music and went to India to study with Ravi Shankar, the foremost sitar player in the world. Harrison studied for eight weeks and came away with enough background to change the complexion of rock music.

Soon afterward, the Beatles recorded in England an album called "Revolver." The resonant sound of the stringed sitar was also introduced on the Beatles' single "Norwegian Wood" (a British pseudonym for marijuana). Overnight the sitar became one of the most popular instruments used to perform rock music. The dissonant strains of Eastern tone intervals became frequent sounds to rock audiences. These sounds, which had their origin 2,000 years ago in *Vedic* hymns, had become commercially popular. The significant point here is this: For the first time in modern history, the Western ear was becoming attuned to Eastern music. It was happening through the medium of rock and roll. With this interest came an interest in the clothing and customs of India. The next step was the introduction of Hindu religious concepts. Thus the Beatles were used as agents to alter the religious structure of an entire Western generation.

Is this not incredible? In 1962 the Beatles were an unknown rock and roll combo performing in dingy nightclubs of Liverpool, England. In the fall of 1963 they spectacularly burst upon the international scene. The idolatrous manner in which teenagers followed them seemed to me too significant to dismiss as just another fad of singing idols. As early as 1964 I predicted that the Beatles would eventually reveal themselves within a religious frame of reference. Those who were skeptical at this postulation have since watched this "prophecy" come true.

When LSD became popular, the Beatles joined the band wagon and led the parade. Their songs took a permissive view of drugs. All four admitted to having taken LSD trips. When Mick Jagger of the Rolling Stones was indicted on a charge of possession of marijuana the Beatles took out a full-page ad in the **London Times** advocating the legalization of marijuana. But eventually the drug scene grew less novel and they began looking elsewhere in search of something to give meaning to their lives. Allen Ginsberg described their plight by saying, "The Beatles satiated every fantasy in relation to the material universe and realized that in order to go any further they would have to go into inner space.

Ringo, the drummer, declared, "We have got almost anything money can buy. Then you look for something else. We have found that something. It fills the gap."

That "something" was transcendental meditation as propagated by the Hindu priest Maharishi Mahesh

Yogi. It thus became logical for the Beatles to embrace Hinduism. George Harrison convinced the other three Beatles to exploit every thing from the burning of incense to the study of Hindu mythology. Harrison had his minicar painted with Indian symbols. On the roof he reproduced an 18th century Hindu painting of the sun in a gold rectangle. One of the doors of his car he covered with the picture of a boar, supposed to be the Hindu god Vishnu in his third reincarnation.

In a television interview with David Frost, Harrison asserted, "I believe in reincarnation. Life and death are only relative to thought. I believe in rebirth. You keep coming back until you have got it straight. The ultimate thing is to manifest divinity and become one with the Creator."

John Lennon was even more adamant in his belief that the Beatles had at least found the answer. He said, "We are going to use all the power we have to spread meditation."

The Beatles are by no means the first Westerners to sample the religions of the East. The mystic practice of yoga was originally introduced to the American public at the beginning of this century by Vivekananda, one of the original disciples of Ramakrishna, a man whose life I will discuss in chapter three. In 1894, Vivekananda founded the Vedanta Society of New York City—the first official Hindu center in the United States. Interest in the cult grew, and by 1930 more than a million citizens of the United States held membership in Eastern religious sects. High in the hills of California's rugged Big Sur country, one hundred and sixty miles north of San Francisco, the nation's first and only Zen Buddhist monastery still flourishes with more activitiy today than ever before.

Indian religious thought has influenced the thinking of such prominent people as Ralph Waldo Emerson, Walt Whitman, Henry David Thoreau, and Mary Baker Eddy who founded the Church of Christ, Scientist. Indians themselves have exported Hinduism to the West with missionary zeal. For centuries, Great Britain had imposed upon India the doctrines of the Christian faith; now Indians are turning the tables on their former conquerors by proselytizing the West.

The Beatles did not start something new. They merely reinforced what already existed, even though Hinduism had lain dormant until their much publicized interest caused the heathen religion to sprout and grow in the West.

One of the prophets of transcendental meditation is Maharishi Mahesh Yogi. This curious little man, full of giggles and sporting a sleepy grin, was a student in Northern India when he saw his *guru* (spiritual teacher) Shankaracharya Brajmananda in a religious parade. The Maharishi testified that he was enlightened by the experience. He joined the monastery of his *guru* and studied in seclusion with the holy man for thirteen years. Before Shankaracharya died in 1953 he gave the Maharishi a refined and simplified system of transcendental meditation and told him his mission was to spread it throughout the world.

The Maharishi first came to the United States in 1959 to establish several groups which are still vigorously functioning and which now form the backbone of his organization here. During the following nine years, he made nine journeys around the world, setting up meditation centers in many cities.

While visiting Singapore in 1968, I learned that the Maharishi's Spiritual Regeneration Movement has had a center for meditation there since 1959. But in Singapore, as in many other parts of the world, the Maharishi had been just another Hindu holy man. But that was before the summer of 1967 when the British Beatles catapulted him to popularity overnight.

It happened in London where the Maharishi had arrived on one of his annual world tours. George Harrison heard about the visit and took John and Paul to hear the lecture. On the following day they added Ringo to their party and took a train to Bangor, Wales to participate in a week long seminar the Maharishi had arranged. Also present were Mick Jagger of the Rolling Stones and his adulterous girlfriend Marianne Faithfull.

The ceremony was long and pompous, involving many flowers. Instantly Maharishi Mahesh Yogi became a spiritual leader not only to the Beatles but to millions of teenagers all over the world as well. He quite frankly attributed the popular success of his Spiritual Regeneration Movement to his long haired English students and referred to them as the "blessed leaders of the world's youth."

(The Beatles have since disavowed the commercial

tactics of the wandering Maharishi but they do not
dispute his authenticity as a holy man. The Beatles
insist that his brand of transcendental meditation
is of great value. George Harrison says, "We are finished with him but we have not broken with the
thoughts of meditation. We have only broken with the
Maharishi and his ideas of making the whole thing
subject to mass media." Ringo adds, "I'm still one hundred per cent for meditation.")

Bearing the stamp of endorsement by the Beatles,
the Maharishi returned to the United States where
he was welcomed by 2,000 people at the Los Angeles
International Airport. He addressed an overflow
audience at the Santa Monic Civic Auditorium. The
next day he spoke privately with Donovan, Mick
Jagger, several members of The Grateful Dead, and
the Jefferson Airplane, an audience which drew into
the circle other prominent rock entertainers. Tommy
Boyce, a composer of many rock and roll hits, admitted
that he had been meditating for nearly three years. "I
started with the Maharishi when he was doing the
same thing for ten people that he is now doing for
ten thousand," he explained.

When the Maharishi spoke in Berkeley, California,
he told an audience of 4,000 that "the youth of this
age has a tool in his hand whereby he can shape this
wretched world into a golden world. That tool is
transcendental meditation." He assured them that to
enjoy the fullest measure of blessing they were not
required to have faith or to renounce liquor, women,
or riotous living.

Appearing on the nationally televised "Johnny Carson Tonight Show," the Maharishi explained what transcendental meditation is all about: "Beyond thought and beyond matter there exists the absolute unity in which all creation originates and which at its purest level constitutes only truth, light and joy. The absolute can be found within every man's consciousness," he said. "By reaching for it, for at least half an hour in the morning and afternoon, a man can gain many benefits."

The mystic assured his followers that anybody could become adept at meditation in the space of four days. The price of initiation into his movement would be thirty-five dollars for college students and a week's salary for adults. At the initiation ceremony each candidate would be required to present six fresh flowers, a new white handkerchief, and two pieces of fruit.

His followers became so enthusiastic about the Maharishi that some believed he could actually work miracles if he so chose. **Look** magazine in April of 1968 declared him to be "the single greatest influence on the young and their music." Thus, an obscure Hindu priest attained world-wide popularity because a rock and roll group elected to sit at his feet.

Back in India, Maharishi Mahesh Yogi set up his *ashram* (retreat or religious academy) in the town of Rishikesh about one hundred and twenty-eight miles north of New Delhi. In January, 1968, the Beatles went there to spend several weeks and to study more thoroughly transcendental meditation.

At that time I was embarking on a 'round-the-world' evangelistic tour that would take me to India while the Beatles were there. I made arrangements to conduct three weeks of private research which would involve hundreds of miles of travel to all parts of India. I was determined to find out for myself what transcendental meditation is all about and what its relationship to Hinduism and the hippies could mean for the youth of America in years to come.

CHAPTER THREE

Calcutta —

Seat of Meditation

During a press conference late 1967, the Monkees were asked their opinion of the hippies.

"Beautiful!" one of them exclaimed. "everyone should wear flowers."

With that, the Monkees began to chant in unison: "*Hare Krishna Hare Krishna, Krishna, Krishna, Hare Hare, Hare Rama, Hare Rama, Rama, Rama, Hare Hare.*"

This was the same Ramakrishna chant I had heard hippies intone while they were "doing their thing." Even more recently, the Broadway musical "Hair" (the first Broadway production to publicly exploit nudity) has aided in the popularization of this chant. Words from the chant comprise the lyrics of one of the major tunes from the show. In the spring of 1969 the soundtrack album of "Hair" (containing a three-minute rendition of the Ramakrishna chant) catapulted to the position of the top-selling album in the world. What does it all mean?

Hare is the name of Vishnu, the Hindu god who offers delightful pleasure. He is referred to as "The Protector." *Rama* is the incarnation of Vishnu as the "Prince of Responsibility." *Krishna* is the "God-narrator" of the *Bhagavadad-Gita,* the sacred text of Hinduism.

To faithful Hindus, the chant is literally the incarnation of the different names, or aspects, of the Hindu god. It is used as a *mantra,* especially at public gatherings, as a stimulus to "give people a common focus for their energies," to quote a hippie. *Ramakrishna* is also the name of a 19th century Hindu holy man considered by some Indians to be their greatest prophet and saint.

Maharishi Mahesh Yogi bases his system of transcendental meditation on the meditation techniques of Ramakrishna, who spent the greater part of his life in the temple-garden of Dakshineswar near Calcutta on the bank of the Ganges. To launch my search into the full significance of Hinduism and the implications of meditation I began at the logical place—Calcutta.

If ever there were a hell on earth, Calcutta would be that place. Never could I have comprehended the extent of poverty and filth that I found there. Two generations ago its population was two million people. Today, overrun by refugees from the British partition, the city is teeming with nine million souls.

As my plane landed in Calcutta my introduction to India was abrupt and terrifying. My diary notes: "My first impression is one of absolute horror and shock. Never could I have comprehended such poverty and filth. I cannot believe what I am seeing here. No words can describe it fully. The sight of sidewalks being used for public toilets, 'sacred' cattle roaming everywhere, and thousands of people lying half-dead in the streets —all this is too much for my eyes, which have seen only the affluence of America."

For many hours I suffered from the reactions of cultural shock. Every environmental stimulus was alien. All that I saw, smelled and heard made me feel like the citizen of another world. In a manner of speaking, I was in "another world." The clean streets of America seemed far, far away. The charm of India, about which I had heard so much, seemed only to be a mixture of despair and fatalism reflected on the face of every person I met. I felt as though I had arrived at the end of the earth. The conditions were a hundred times worse than anything I have ever seen in Harlem or Chicago's South Side.

Most of the automobiles on Calcutta streets are taxis. Small cars based on British automotive design, they are *Hindusthans*.

I hailed one of them and directed the driver to the residence of a missionary friend with whom I would be staying. As we wound our way through the listless mobs of human beings I studied the faces of the people. An estimated seventeen per cent of the nine million people in Greater Calcutta have no home. Their only dwelling place is a slab of concrete sidewalk where they lie hour after hour, curled up in a filthy blanket.

As we drew near to the downtown section, the crowds grew thicker. "Teeming" seems to be an inadequate adjective to describe the throngs within range of my gaze. Whenever my car stopped at an intersection, emaciated children with bodies twisted from hunger would run up to the window. Rubbing their bloated stomachs and gesturing toward their mouths, they would cry out, "Money, *Sahib* (their word for gentleman or master) !"

Looking out another window I could see a man with one leg. The other had been crudely amputated. He was lying half-dead on the curb while a constant stream of people passed by. His glazed eyes gave mute testimony that death was only a matter of minutes away. He mattered little to the passersby. They scarcely noticed him. The truck would pick up his carcass in the morning and throw him unceremoniously onto the heap of wasted bodies.

Such disregard for human life, I was to discover later, is typical of the Indian's fatalistic attitude fostered by Hinduism. Over against such callousness the compassion, love and human dignity engendered by the teachings of Jesus Christ stood in bold relief. Such are the blessed foundations of our Western civilizations.

Our taxi sped on, and we passed by a building that was being erected by "coolie" labor. These fantastic people would balance a dozen bricks on their heads and climb up two stories on a crude ladder to the mason. They worked for twelve to fourteen hours a day and earned the equivalent of fifty cents for their effort. This would buy them enough rice to stay alive for another day of the same tortuous work. I wanted to photograph the scene, but my driver warned me not to. Indians would strongly resent a foreigner's photographing a disadvantaged section of the city, he said.

What a relief it was to arrive at the mission compound. I stumbled from the taxi dazed and bewildered as missionary Mark Buntain and his wife greeted me. These dear people had willingly made Calcutta their home in order to bring Christ to a nation bound by heathenism. They had my admiration and profound respect.

That night before I retired I summarized the events of the day in a brief letter home:

Dear Mom and Dad:

There is simply no way to describe what I have seen today. I don't think even pictures could convey the scenes that have made me sick inside. A stench pervades the Calcutta air. I have knelt in prayer many times to thank God for having been raised in Christian America, but until now I never really knew what thankfulness was.

Eat a good meal tonight, and lie down on clean linen with freedom from fear and want. But before you go to sleep, in the best way you know how, thank God for the blessings of America.

Your son,
Bob

I lay on my bed for a long time that first night, staring out the window and listening to the sounds of the city.

"Why must India be like this?" I asked myself. The next three weeks would answer the question for me. Hinduism was directly and indirectly responsible for most of the suffering I had witnessed. Before I would leave this second most populous land on earth I would see paganism in its rawest forms. I would learn to dispise nearly everything the mistaken hippies stand for. I was to learn in vivid confrontation all that transcendental meditation really represents.

Morning came, and I was up at 5:30 to watch the missionaries feed the starving children. With allotments from Christian relief agencies, the mission dispenses several cans of milk a day to hungry urchins who gather there each morning.

The sun had barely risen when the first contingent of youngsters appeared. They ranged in age from two to ten, but each would get only one cup of milk for the day. They streamed into the compound from all parts of the city, some walking miles to reach the source of their only food for the day.

Like children everywhere, they were noisy and restless, except those in tattered rags who huddled together in the chill morning air to stay warm. Many of them had no parents ... no home. They spend the precious days of their childhood roaming the streets from one garbage pile to another in relentless search for food.

After more than six hundred children had come, the gates were closed. My heart was rent with sadness as I watched those who were shut out pleading for life-giving milk to fill their tin cups. My mind went back to those days as a child when I had complained because my parents made me eat something full of nutrition that I didn't like.

"God, forgive me!" I mumbled through tears of compassion and helpless pity.

That evening one of the young men in the mission church invited me to his house for dinner. We met at the compound and walked for a good many blocks on narrow streets, passing one hovel after another. Finally we arrived at his "home." It was a dwelling constructed of cheap, thin boards with no paint and few refinements. The "door" was a ragged blanket hanging in the entrance. The interior consisted of one room, ten by twenty feet, which accommodated a table, two beds, and a stove. In this postage-stamp home he lived with his parents and two sisters and a brother. His father worked at the airport unloading cargo for one of the airlines. He earned fifty dollars a month—extremely good wages in Calcutta.

These impoverished friends proudly displayed for me the most prized possession of the household: a small record player with a sizeable stack of rock and roll recordings. Most of the records were cut by American artists popular a decade earlier. There were several more recent records of a Bombay rock band and a couple of albums featuring the Beachboys. Somehow, even the Jefferson Airplane managed to find its way to this filth laden hut in a Calcutta slum.

Our dinner began with soup that had been cooked in an unwashed pan. I knew well the consequences of eating food that had been improperly washed or cooked, Consequently, my prayer of thanksgiving took on added significance!

After the first course came the main entree—a piece of something fried to a leathery slab. I cut a piece to eat, trying to appear as nonchalant as possible, while I fought off the sickened look that must have crept over my face. After taking several bites I made the mistake of asking what I was eating.

"Cow's tongue!" came the eager reply.

To my host it was a delicacy saved for special occasions. To me it only conjured up images of half-starved brahma cattle foraging in garbage piles I had seen along Calcutta streets. My imagination suggested that the cow that once belonged to this tongue had died from starvation or disease and had been carted off to the butcher shop from the gutter.

I smiled, assuring my friends that the meat was very tasty and asking the Lord to forgive me for stretching the truth just a little on their behalf.

Excusing myself from dinner, I hurried back to the mission compound to retire early. The next day I was to make my long-awaited visit to the Ramakrishna temple.

After breakfast I hailed a taxi and directed him to the temple. My driver was a Sikh, identified by his beard and turban. The Sikhs are a religious sect of Hinduism who never cut their hair. These men always carry a long knife concealed on their person. It is the custom that whenever the knife is drawn, blood must be shed before it is sheathed again. I would use the services of this taxi for the entire day and it would cost me only two dollars.

Our journey to the temple took about an hour. We passed through downtown Calcutta where a herd of goats had strayed. The weather had turned warm and scenes of the city were constantly changing ... an Indian cricket game on an open square ... two old men rummaging through a pile of garbage ... a branch of the Ganges flowing through the city on its way to the Bay of Bengal ...

Finally we crossed a bridge over the Ganges to the side where the temple is located. Actually, I had been traveling through the better parts of Calcutta. Now the streets were becoming more narrow and the sewage system was an open dirt ditch running in front of the shacks. The per capita income in India is only seventy dollars anually; seventy per cent of the population is illiterate. I had learned these statistics, but I did not grasp their full meaning until I saw them translated into human form and viewed for myself the thousands of homeless, ragged nameless figures sleeping in the streets and alleys of this dismal city.

I found other countries of Asia that were nearly as poor as India. But India's plight surpasses them all. One obvious reason is that the Indians are a solemn people. They seldom complain about their disadvantaged condition. This stoicism is a heritage of Hinduism. When something goes wrong, the Indian blames it on sins he committed in a previous existence. Christian principles that undergird Western societies are non-existent in India.

As I peered through the windows of the taxi a sense of frustration gripped me. I had been taught that life is of supreme value, but before me were endless numbers of faceless crowds enduring suffering on a large scale, hungry, crying out for help but there was nothing I could do about it. Compassion began turning to offense and indignation at the heathen philosophies that were responsible for this environment.

My taxi stopped several hundred yards from the Ramakrishna temple. I told the driver to wait for me.

A five minute walk brought me to the temple grounds. The main structure was the temple, of course, located in the center of the area with several smaller buildings surrounding it. These were the residences of the *swamis*. The quiet and peaceful atmosphere was in sharp contrast to the bustle of downtown Calcutta. The grounds were clean and neatly trimmed, and I was surprised at seeing a place outside the mission compound where filth did not prevail.

I stepped inside what appeared to be the headquarters and asked if I could speak with someone who could instruct me in meditation. Ten minutes passed, then a robed *swami* (the equivalent of a celibate monk) entered the room. I explained to him my quest to find out all I could about the art of meditation. His soft-spoken manner and considerate attention belied the fact that he was an important representative of paganism.

"Before we discuss meditation," he said, "it is essential that you first have a basic understanding of Hinduism."

I admitted my inadequate grasp of the religion and asked him to explain it to me as time permitted.

"Certainly!" he replied.

My host began by informing me that Hinduism is considered to be the oldest religion of civilization, dating back further than traditional religions. Elements of the sect were brought to India, he said, from Aryan invaders from the north. The three chief gods are Brahma, Vishnu, and Shiva, although Brahma is generally considered to be the supreme god.

The figure of 330 million gods to be worshipped by Hindus is not the sum of an actual count but is intended to suggest infinity and represent the hundreds of Hindu deities.

Hinduism is at once a theology, a philosophy, a social system, and a way of life. Consequently, nearly every act of a pious Hindu involves some sort of ritual. Various sects have different practices but all Hindus believe in some form of reincarnation.

"A discussion of Yoga and the caste systems would be very time-consuming," my *swami* friend told me, "so just let me go on with the basic points of Hinduism."

He continued his detailed explanation: "The Vedanta" (the official name of the Hindu religion), he said, "is the philosophy which has evolved from the spiritual experiences of great sages embodied in the four Veda—the oldest scriptures in the world."

"The basic teaching of the Vedanta," my mentor related, "says that the real nature of man is divine, and the aim of every individual on earth is to try to unfold the divinity which is inherent in him."

The *swami* denied the existence of evil. "Evil men are just those in a lesser stage of spiritual development," he explained. "Remember. God is in you. God is in everything. The idea of God as a personal deity is the result of ignorance of one's own real nature, which is divine."

He outlined for me the Hindu creed by stating: "Any sincere belief is enough because the basic truths of all religions are the same. The Vedanta accepts all religions of the world and honors all great prophets and teachers of humanity. After all," he said, "spirituality is only a state of mind."

"Let me tell you something about the Ramakrishna movement in particular," he continued. "The life of Ramakrishna expressed, to a greater degree than that of any other teacher, the Vadantic idea of religious universality. After many years of meditation he realized his identity with the God-head. But this did not satisfy him. He then proceeded to test the universality of his experience by following the paths of Islam and Christianity. Thus, toward the end of his life, he was able to say with absolute authority that all religions are true and that the ultimate reality could be known by a member of any sect if he or she persued the ideal with devotion and sincerity. It was then that Jesus and Allah appeared to him in a vision and told him that meditation was the answer to all the world's problems. Ramakrishna has told us to worship God as a universal power rather than any specific god. We're sort of a 'spiritual United Nations,' seeking to unite all religions of the world through meditation."

At this point I said to my teacher, "I'm interested in finding out something about transcendental meditation. What can you tell me about it?"

He laughed. "I suppose you've heard about Maharishi Mahesh Yogi," he said. "Since he has become popular, many people have been wanting to find out about meditation. I must admit that most of us here at the Ramakrishna temple don't approve of the commercial techniques he uses. But I'll be happy to tell you what his meditation system is all about."

"Meditation is based upon repetition of the *Mantra*. Actually, *mantras* have been of great importance in Hindu schools. Traditionally, a *mantra* is a sacred text, or even a syllable taken from our scriptures, whose vibrations harmonize with your own. It is believed to give mystical powers to the person who pronounces it in a proper spirit. In one sense, it is a sound with supernatural properties. It is given by a teacher to a pupil and most often to be kept secret and recited aloud when alone or silently with the lips or only mentally. It must be recited continually until the mind's activities become fixed around the *mantra*."

Suddenly he turned to me and asked, "Are you a Christian?"

"Yes," I replied.

"Then you know where it says in the Gospel of John, '... And the word became flesh ...' Like that, *mantras* are believed to have creative power. Some Hindu schools teach that the beginning of the world was an emanation of a Vedic word, or words, originally pronounced by Brahma. For that reason, these words are now holy and indestructible. The *mantra* is an active symbol of a particular diety and if a person meditates and repeats a *mantra* enough while making an effort to identify himself with it, the meditator becomes one with the deity. For example, one who sings Shiva's name becomes Shiva himself. Let me quote you a sample of a *mantra*."

In a monotonous tone the *swami* recited the following, his eyes shut as he said: "My homage to Shiva, the gentle, the one Cause of three causes, to Thee I surrender myself. You are my resort, O great Lord."

He then opened his eyes and said, "If I had concentrated enough on what I was just saying I would have become Shiva myself. Normally one's spiritual entities are directed outward. Meditation turns them inward and releases the spiritual potential within each of us. We can thus become identified with the God of the *mantra*."

I pondered the significance of what the *swami* had told me. The gods worshipped by the Hindus are false gods—actually, they are demon spirits. The essence of the *mantra* is an invitation to a demon spirit to take control of one's faculties. Perhaps that explains why Mike Love, the lead singer of the Beachboys, said that when he meditated sexual images came to his mind ... "on a very gross level," he admitted.

I thanked the *swami* for his time and for the information, then made my exit. Before leaving the grounds

I went to the temple, an imposing structure several stories high. As custom dictated, I removed my shoes before stepping inside. The interior was beautifully decorated with sculptures and paintings representing Hindu gods. At one end of the temple was a life-size idol of Ramakrishna. Approximately two dozen Indians, poorly dressed and obviously poorly fed, were bowing and touching their heads to the floor as they tossed what little money they had at the feet of the idol. The intense, pagan idolatry of the Ramakrishna movement was vividly portrayed.

I watched as the worshippers sought in vain sincerity to please the inanimate idol of stone. Tears formed in my eyes. The Bible, in the seventeenth chapter of the Acts, says that when the Apostle Paul looked on the city of Athens and saw it given to idolatry he was stirred in his spirit. I felt what must have been that same stirring as the Holy Spirit gripped my heart.

Walking from the temple I glanced at the literature the *swami* had given me. It contained lines from the *Bhagavadad-Gita,* the Celestial song of Hindu theology. One line described the perfect disciple as one "who sees me in all, and sees all in me, for him I am not lost, and he is not lost for me."

I recalled how George Harrison of the Beatles had mentioned that his *mantra* appeared in Lennon's song "I Am the Walrus." The first line from that song is this: "I am he, as you are he, as you are me, and we are all together." That line represents essentially the same thought as contained in the Hindu sacred text, the *Bhagavadad-Gita.*

I was also reminded of Mick Jagger of the Rolling Stones, who had considered the possibility of recording a *mantra* with the Beatles and Allen Ginsberg on a 45-rpm disc which could be played in jukeboxes. I thanked God that He had allowed my search to uncover the true meaning of meditation and of the *mantra*. If Satan were going to introduce the youth of America to Hinduism he had chosen his prophets well. Who, besides the Beatles and other prominent rock musicians, could have the influence and means to sway the religious beliefs of the youth of our land?

I vowed to God that when I returned to America I would write a book exposing the Satanic nature of what the hippies and the Beatles were trying to accomplish.

"If the Beatles are going to pray to Hindu gods, invite demon spirits to enter and control their bodies and encourage America's youth to do likewise," I thought, "where might it all lead?"

My search was not yet over. The question still remained to be answered.

CHAPTER IV

Banaras – The

Hindu Mecca

In Europe during my voyage to India I chanced to meet a hippie at the Rome airport and fell into conversation with him. This disciple of mysticism urged me to include in my itinerary a trip to the Hindu holy city of Banaras. "No trip to India would be complete without it," he said, "for there in one spot you can see all of the scenes commonly associated with India."

Since I was intent upon finding out all I could about Hinduism I decided to visit Banaras, allegedly the second oldest city in the world (next to Damascus) and the greatest cultural and religious center in India.

When my sojourn in Calcutta had ended, I boarded an Indian Airways plane that would take me to my destination five hundred miles north. I found Banaras clustered on the west bank of the Ganges River, bounded on the northern and southern suburbs by two other rivers. Its population is seven hundred thousand —small by Indian standards. The city abounds in historic tradition. Hindus believe that the gods chose

44

Banaras to initiate the first spark of humanity. Indeed, history points to this spot as the site of some of the earliest endeavors of the civilized world. The entire city is dedicated to Shiva. The faithful make pilgrimages to this city, looking on its environs as the holiest spot on earth.

All the activities of this metropolis revolve around the Ganges. The "sacred" river begins at the foot of the Himalayas which is said to be the home of Shiva. During the summer monsoon season the Ganges may swell to a width of a mile or more, but during the winter season it is only a few hundred yards wide. To this river every morning thousands of Hindus come to bathe and to worship.

I arrived during the winter season and immediately checked in at the Clark Hotel. The desk clerk suggested that the first thing I should do was to take a morning cruise down the Ganges. Without much prompting he quickly arranged for a guide to pick me up the following morning at 5:30. To a travel-weary pilgrim that sounded too early, but I was determined to cram as many sights and experiences into my memory as possible so I readily agreed.

My room, by Indian standards, was quite nice. But then one might expected an improvement in a "holy" city! The best hotel accommodations in Calcutta come complete with roaches and plenty of dirt. They cannot be compared even with the worst hotel accommodations in an American city.

I had stayed with missionaries in Calcutta so my room there had been clean. But bathing in Calcutta was another matter. The water ran only twice a day and had to be collected in a tub for washing later. To "shower" you stood in the tub and dipped the water up and poured it over your head. The water supply was unfit for drinking or even for brushing the teeth.

But here in Banaras I found that the food was not only edible, it was actually quite palatable! The total price for room, three meals a day and two teas was less than eight dollars at the rate of official exchange.

At sunrise I arose and joined my eager guide. The city was already alive with people as we drove into the heart of this notable urban complex. Literally thousands of people were already enroute to the Ganges for their daily dip for purposes of spiritual restoration.

My guide finally parked the car and we set out on foot through the business section toward the Ganges. On the bank of the river, blasting into the ears of the devout Hindus was the loudspeaker of a communist. The man stood there bombarding the ears of his fellow Indians with the virtues of communism as we shouldered our way through. At the edge of the water my guide beckoned to a young lad who would serve as "row power" for our boat.

I inspected the craft and immediately began to wonder about its ability to carry us all above the water.

"It won't sink," my guide assured me. "But if it does, Banaras would be a wonderful place to die."

Any indictment against Hinduism in that environment would have been unwise, so I mutely disputed his statement—even thought my host was a Muslim.

We rowed first to the center of the river so we didn't have to navigate through a sea of bathers along the shore. As we paddled upstream, the sun had risen over the eastern bank enough to dispel the thick mist that clung to the river.

Far out in the river I looked back and saw the skyline of Banaras taking shape. Mud huts mingled with massive palaces; turrets, towers and minarets jutted skyward. The walls of many houses were spotched with dung patties that had been plastered there and left to dry in the sun. Later it would be used for fuel.

For nearly five miles along the western bank of the Ganges leading out from the city one could see the *ghats* (landings or steps). On these strange foundations were built big bamboo canopies by the thousands that sheltered countless numbers of professional priests and their devotional clients. These priests served not only as the custodians of the dry clothes and purses of the bathers, they also provided combs, mirrors and materials for offering a blessing on their devotees. Many of the priests, as well as the laymen, had their arms and foreheads decorated with the trident sign of Shiva.

The Beatles, with the exception of Ringo, had taken the ceremonial bath in the Ganges near the *ashram* of Maharishi Mahesh Yogi. This event made me all the more curious to find out what the bathing signified.

Now as I looked toward the ghats, thousands of people shed their clothes and walked waist deep into the waters of the Ganges. Men and women stood side by side—many in the nude. They clasped their hands in a gesture of prayer and dipped several times in the holy river. This would be followed by prayer and meditation. I turned to my guide for an explanation.

"Hindus believe that the sun is the symbol of ultimate truth," he explained. "Their religion commands them to pray before the sun because it is the foremost physical manifestation of the Divine creative power." He shot at me a rhetorical question: "Where would man be if there were no sun?

The Muslim continued: "Human beings are produced and supported by the sun. So, the Hindus believe the sun is a manifestation of the true consciousness of God. Therefore, because the sun is the giver of life, they adore and worship the sun. Their act of devotion accomplishes two things: The proper worship of the sun and the worship of the river goddess. During the ritual *Kumbha Mela* more than four million Hindus will crowd the banks to do just what you have seen many people doing this morning."

So, I thought to myself, *the Beatles were actually performing the ritual of sun-worship!* I was sufficiently disturbed by the heathen practices that I had observed but became downright angry when I realized that these men and their hippie brothers were intent upon importing these same pagan ideas to America.

The bathers there in the Ganges that morning were soon joined by people seeking better health by performing breathing exercises and other feats of gymnastics. Despite the cool temperature of the morning the Hindus showed little regard for physical discomfort. Those who had finished their bathing sat on the *ghats* meditating. Others were worshipping phallic symbols

—representations of the male sex organs—constructed near the water.

It should be noted that into the waters in which the Indians were bathing is poured all of the sewage from the city of seven hundred thousand people. And at this spot the remains of more than fifty human bodies a day are dumped into the river, to say nothing of all the dead cattle which seem to abound in India. I watched in misery as Hindus filled large pots with water from the putrid river and heartily drank its contents.

When they had finished their bathing rituals and meditation many of the people would take home several buckets full of Ganges water to use for cooking and drinking purposes. They worship the river, so they have no fear whatever of disease from the water. It is little wonder that thousands of people are frequently killed by rampaging epidemics that systematically sweep through a community. Such situations bring into vivid contrast the difference between Hinduism and Christianity.

After we had sailed about three miles upstream I inquired concerning the burning *ghats* where the dead are cremated. My guide consented to show me one of those sites and we began rowing in that direction.

Essential to the doctrines of Hinduism is the belief in reincarnation. Life to them is a series of cycles in which the soul comes back to earth in various forms depending upon determining factors in one's previous existence.

The most important *ghat* is called *manikarnika*. With fond hopes of being cremated on this spot, many Hindus live out their late years in Banaras where they will be blessed by Shiva, the Hindu god of death, and then pass directly to nirvana. Cremation is necessary to the Hindus as a means of preventing the soul from returning to inhabit the dead body.

The entire process involves an elaborate ritual. Unless it is performed properly the sub-conscious of the dead person is said to remain in the world of spirits and ghosts. These haunt the place of his former abode and people who had been his acquaintances. It is this strong belief in the need for precise ritual that prevents the Hindus from adopting electric crematoriums which would certainly be more efficient and sanitary.

Within one or two hours after the person is pronounced dead, his body is carried to a burning ghat by male members of his family. The one exception to this ritual is the victim who has died from cholera or smallpox. In such cases, some Hindus are afraid the germs which caused the disease might be reincarnated ancestors so they refuse to properly destroy the body. Instead, they toss it into the holy Ganges.

As we rowed up to burning ghat, preparations were under way for the cremation of a two-month-old boy. The body was first dipped in the water to "purify" it and then left to dry while a funeral pyre of wood was built. The head of the body to be cremated is usually shaved clean, but in this instance the shave was not necessary. The dead child was placed on top of the pyre and butter was spread on it to facilitate the burning process. The fires usually require from three to four hours to consume a normal, healthy body. But this baby was gone in only about an hour. The fire had been lit by the chief mourner—probably the child's father—as he stood without emotion watching the flames take away the unfortunate victim. Then its ashes were thrown to their final resting place in softly flowing waters of the Ganges.

My guide told me that if a cremation takes place far from the Ganges the navel of the body is kept until a member of the family makes a pilgrimage to Banaras at which time it is thrown into the river.

The next cremation I observed was that of an elderly man. The members of his family haggled with the priest before setting the price of cremation at twenty rupees (about three U.S. dollars). While I was waiting for the preparation of the pyre I walked around the area near the ghat and spotted a Hindu holy man intent on his meditation. Before him was a pile of fresh cow dung. He was seated in a squatted position staring at his index finger which he had extended directly in front of his nose. He had a strange, demonic look on his face. He appeared to be Satan incarnated. I asked another priest what the man was doing.

"He is worshipping cow dung," was the simple reply. "The cow gives milk and milk gives life and so the cow is holy. Whatever comes out of the cow is holy. Therefore, we worship cow's dung."

The whole sight might have been amusing, but I

found the spiritual connotation of the whole affair repulsive.

Just then my guide hurried up to announce the start of the next cremation. When it appeared that the dead man's body was dry from his ceremonial dip in the river, the priest chanted some prayers over the corpse. Then the dead man's son took some bananas and other fruit and squashed them into a mash which was placed in the mouth of the dead man for his soul's journey after death. With no expression of grief or sorrow, the son then took a torch and set fire to the pyre of logs. The flames engulfed the body as the surviving son stood watching.

Until the government put a stop to the practice, widows would often practice "suttee" by throwing themselves on the burning body of their husbands to die with them.

I walked away from the pyre that day with the stench of burning flesh still in my nostrils, stunned by what I had witnessed. If my predictions hold true, the false religion of the last days will be based in part on oriental mysticism. Could it be that Western societies will begin to adopt cremation as a means of disposing of dead bodies? Not enough hippies have died yet for such a ritual to become popular or for the movement to formulate a collective philosophy of death. However, in keeping with their acceptance of the doctrine of reincarnation it is reasonable to assume that cremation will become another of their folkways. If George Harrison has given burial instructions in his will, I am certain that those instructions include the act of cremation. Perhaps the other Beatles have all followed suit.

Nauseated and heartsick, I asked my guide to take me back to the hotel. Word that an American was in town must have preceded me because a small boy with an Indian elephant and a man with a dromedary (a one-humped creature often incorrectly called a camel) hailed me and begged me to ride their beasts. A student of yoga came and offered to perform twenty-five positions for me. We argued over the price until we reached an agreement on the worth of his demonstration. I was amazed at how he could twist and contort his body. In one position he sucked in his stomach until it appeared to disappear. Fewer than two inches remained between his navel and his spine.

The most fascinating exhibit was the snake charmer. Like most people, I associated this practice with the East and I wasn't disappointed. Exactly as you might imagine, the Indian played his flute and the cobra rose erect from a basket. The charmer insisted the cobra had no fangs, but forty thousand Indians die every year from snake bites and I wasn't going to take any chances.

This man also staged a fight between a cobra and a mongoose. The little mongoose, resembling an oversized rat, is the only animal of its size capable of killing a snake. He moves with lightning speed, so fast the snake can't strike him.

On the lawn of the hotel the man held the mongoose as it eyed a cobra on the grass. Then suddenly he released the mongoose and quicker than the eye could follow the little animal raced across the grass and had

the cobra's head in his teeth. The snake thrashed
furiously and wrapped itself around the mongoose in
an effort to free itself. But in moments it was dead,
yet the mongoose continued to hang on. The snake
charmer picked up the snake by its tail but the mongoose still hung on, dangling in the air. It refused to
give up its grip, as if afraid the snake were only
feigning death.

I paid the charmer his fee and walked back to the
veranda of the hotel. A young hippie girl was trying
to sell some of her paintings to several other foreigners.
She was from Australia but had come to see Maharishi
Mahesh Yogi. Why?

"I want to see what it is that has so interested the
Beatles," she told me.

I inquired concerning this interest and she was eager
to tell me in detail about her conversion to Hinduism.

Haven't you heard?" she asked. "We hippies have
plans to build a Hindu temple in Banaras! We even
have some of the building materials already collected.
Why, we have more hippies in India than you do in
America," she exclaimed with glee. "Right now hippies
from all over the world—especially from Western
Europe—are making pilgrimages to India to convert
to Hinduism. In Southern India we have established an
entire colony with more than three hundred perma-
nent residents already.

I tried to witness to her of Christ, but she was so
enthused about Hinduism that there was no point in
continuing the conversation.

How long will it take, I thought, *before she sees the folly of this kind of life? I wonder who her parents are and if they even know where she is.*

The girl appeared to be only sixteen or seventeen years old. I could not help feeling sorry for her in such a wretched, useless pursuit.

Before I went away she asked, "Have you met any of the hippies in Banaras?"

I told her I had not.

"Well, I'm not surprised," she said. "Most of them are involved in illegal drug rackets and are afraid that any foreigner might be a government official or a spy of some sort. But there are lots of American hippies in Banaras. Most of them live a few miles up the river away from the main part of town. However, there are several houseboats full of French hippies moored near the burning *ghat*."

I pressed her to tell me where I could find hippies in Banaras, but she first made me promise that if I saw any I wouldn't tell them who tipped me off. I promised and bade her goodbye, hoping for her sake she would succeed in selling her paintings.

My guide was still nearby so I asked him to take me to the French hippies at the houseboat near the *ghat*. He wasn't enthusiastic about the idea. Indians don't like the hippies any better than the majority of Americans do.

"All they come here for is to take drugs and use our Indian girls for prostitutes," my guide said angrily.

"They ran a bunch of hippies out of Katmandu, Nepal
a few weeks ago." He thought that's what India should
do also.

I insisted that talking with them was vital for my
research, so he reluctantly consented to show me the
area where they might be found.

Evening shadows were stealing over the city as we
headed back through the center of Banaras toward
the Ganges. We walked down a narrow street lined
with mud huts toward a steep bank of the river. The
steps that were once a part of the *ghat's* superstructure
had been long ago covered with silt.

As we approached the houseboat I could hear in the
distance a tamborine beating rhythm to the erratic
melody of a flute. My guide stopped short, saying he
would meet me at the car. In a flash he was gone.

I stepped onto the houseboat and knocked on the
door. A long-haired young man opened the door or
hatch and hesitantly invited me inside. The compartment was about twenty feet long, six feet wide and
not more than four feet high. I crouched down on the
floor and introduced myself. The Frenchmen all spoke
broken English and wanted to know how I had found
them.

Trying to ignore the question, I surveyed their
"home." A picture of the Hindu god Shiva hung at
one end of the flat and a candle stood burning at the
other. One of the hippies was preparing the evening
meal—five fried potatoes each about the size of
chicken eggs. The hippies were very reluctant to talk

with me at first, but I did learn they were all from
Paris and that at least three of them had come from
wealthy families. The tamborine player informed me
that they had been in Northern India but were now
headed southward.

What brought them to India, I asked. The answer of
the first hippie startled me: "It was influence of
Indian music in rock and roll that first interested me
in the East. I like rock and roll because the music
involves you. You feel like you're part of what is being
played, especially the music from groups like the Fugs
and the Mothers of Invention."

At this point the cook joined in. "We're not Hindus
yet, actually, but we are fascinated by the mysticism
of India." Then he added: "I guess you could say that
we're tired of Western culture. Most of us like it here,
except for the caste and marriage systems. Since we're
all pacifists the non-violent convictions here in India
appeal to us. Compared to the aggressiveness of the
West, the tranquility of India is refreshing."

The flute player stopped his lone recital long enough
to say, "We don't really consider ourselves to be foreigners anyway. We're not really citizens of any country. We all belong to the universal family of mankind."

I began asking the group questions about their
interest in Hinduism. The tamborine player summed
up their feelings this way:

"All I can say is that we have a great deal of respect for the Hindu religion. I guess most of us have

special reverence for the *babutis* or *sadhus*, the Hindu holy men."

This little cluster of hippies was reluctant to talk much further. The flutist especially was suspicious that I was some sort of government agent spying on them. Both *ganja* (the Indian name for marijuana) and *hashish* (a drug similar to marijuana but much stronger) are available through licensed sellers who control the market. However, excessive amounts are still handled under cover through the black market at higher prices.

The correlation of Eastern religions and drugs is more than coincidental. The cult of Shiva has long used marijuana as part of its worship. Indian families drink a marijuana solution on Shiva's birthday. Hindus believe that drugs give them a consciousness of God. Some holy men say that meditation "trips" are are quite similar to acid "trips." Does this mean that the demonic factor present in meditation is also at work in the use of "conscious-expanding" hallucinagens? Perhaps this is why Timothy Leary combines Hinduism with his marijuana cult.

The lack of cordiality shown by the hippies didn't bother me. I hadn't planned to stay long anyhow. Their unkept appearance and the smell of unwashed bodies in close quarters made the group a pitiable, if not a repulsive, sight.

When they finally were convinced that I was not there to try to catch them in possession of drugs, the flutist opened a small pouch of *hashish* and placed it in a small dish. Then he picked up a *chillum* (a funnel-shaped device about six inches long and one and a half inches wide at the largest end). Next he placed a small rock in the *chillum* then poured the drug mixture on top of it. The rock prevented the *hashish* from flowing through the opening in the bottom but allowed smoke to pass through. He lit the drug with a candle's flame at the top of the *chillum* then cupped his hands and mouth around the bottom in order to inhale the fumes. After he had taken a few puffs he passed it around the room. Each took his turn and then handed it to me suggesting that I experience the pleasure of "turning on." I firmly declined, despite their insistence that I join them.

I tried to keep the conversation going, but my friends sank lower and lower into delirium on their way to the never-never world of drugs. Conversation became almost impossible. The sweet fumes from *hashish* now began filling the room. I became light-headed and a little groggy and decided this was the time to leave. I asked if I could take their picture, but they refused—still not altogether certain of my identity.

Suddenly the tamborine player sat up straight. "I don't care if you are a government spy. Give me two rupees and you can take my picture."

He crawled out on the deck and I snapped his picture.

Farewell to a sad and sorry collection of humanity. How good it was to breathe again the fresh air of the open sky!

As I slowly climbed the bank of the Ganges toward

my waiting car I gazed for a moment at the innocent looking houseboat anchored there. Those few French hippies were representative of thousands wandering all over India. Rock and roll music was responsible for directing many of them to the East. I recalled how Keith Richards of the Rolling Stones was caught smoking *hashish* and how the Beatles had then spoken in his defense by advocating the legalization of hallucinagenic drugs. I remembered hearing of the Doors, a popular American rock group, propagandizing the slogan, "Nirvana now!" and knew that their drummer, John Densmore, and guitarist Robby Krieger were Maharishi followers. I recalled too that Bob Wier, guitarist for the Grateful Dead had evaluated transcendental meditation as "the best answer." He added: "It is to us what Jesus was saying 2,000 years ago." I concluded that rock and roll and all of its associated evils would be an increasingly important tool in Satan's hand to destroy the morals of this generation.

I felt deep sympathy as I stood there in the twi-light of India thinking about those French hippies. Perhaps I should have shown them more compassion, those souls so in need of God. But they, like so many of their brothers, had turned their back on God deliberately to follow false gods.

"Maybe I have no right to condemn the Beatles," I thought, but then remembered quickly that they and other rock musicians were directly responsible for the ruined lives in that houseboat and of thousands of other lost souls in the bloom of their youth. How many others were at that moment worshipping Hindu gods and inviting demon spirits into their bodies through the guise of meditation—all because of the Beatles?

A few days before in Calcutta I had picked up a copy of **"The Junior Statesman"**, a magazine published for teenagers in India. The issue I purchased was dedicated to the Beatles. I recalled what I had read in one of its articles: "... can anyone deny that but for the Beatles the Maharishi would not have been known the world over today? Even for most Indians the Beatles discovered the Yogi."

I resolved to be more adamant than ever in my denunciation of those mop-haired Britons—of the slovenly activities of the hippies ... and of the din of rock and roll which had lured so many to their destruction. I longed to spare some teenager the misery that these French hippies will some day experience through their devotion to drugs.

"Oh God!" I cried, looking up to heaven, "There is more than a river bank that separates me from those hippies. It is faith in You that has spared me a life like that. Thank you, Lord, that while these hippies bow in worship to heathen gods I have been fortunate enough to have found your Son, Jesus Christ, as my Saviour! With Your help, I am going to write a book exposing what I have seen here in Banaras. I want the teenagers of America to know what the hippies and the Beatles really stand for. It won't be easy. You know that, Lord. Many people will call me a fanatic and won't listen to the truth about this serious situation. I'll allow nothing to change my mind. *Nothing!*"

I took some paper from my pocket and recorded my

conversation with the hippies in the houseboat. It was getting late. My search would have to continue another day.

I walked slowly away from the Ganges, more determined than ever that Satan had originated the phonomenon called the Beatles ... the hippies ... and the pounding beat of rock and roll. It became clear to me that these were the media to accomplish his purpose of turning the attention of youthful America toward pagan religions.

"Yes, God," I reiterated. "With Your help I will write a book on what I have seen and experienced here."

CHAPTER FIVE

Temples and Torture

One final swing through Banaras yielded for me a Niagara of sights and sounds and information about Hinduism which I shall always remember. I saw the Golden Temple where a phallic emblem (or *lingam* as it may be called) is worshipped as a representation of Shiva ... the Durga Temple where dozens of monkeys thrive as objects of worship by the Hindus ... the Hindu University—largest residential university in the East—and Sarnath, the spot where Buddha preached his first sermon and initiated his original disciples.

Upon leaving Banaras, I traveled 400 miles northwestward, to the city of Agra. This city is host to the most beautiful of all buildings, the Taj Mahal.

The city was not as accommodating to me, however, because I learned at the airport that the two best Agra hotels were filled. An official recommended that I take a room at the third-rate Grand Hotel. But knowing the calibre of India's best I was not eager to settle for number three, nevertheless I agreed quickly because I had no choice.

As expected, I found my room complete with the usual roaches, lack of running water and filth. At dawn I went directly to the Clark Hotel, discovered I had to entrain for New Delhi one hundred and twenty-five miles away to catch my plane so I visited the Taj Mahal enroute to the train depot.

Built by Shah Jahan to enshrine the remains of his wife, the shimmering white marble monument is considered to be the finest tribute to a couple's love ever built. It appeared to be larger than I had expected. The splendor of its inlaid gems stood out in vivid contrast to the poverty apparent everywhere in India. Twenty thousand workmen had labored for twenty-two years to complete it in 1653 A.D. at a cost of seventy million dollars.

I left the scene of the Taj Mahal in a rickshaw for a thirty-minute ride to the train station then rode for four hours of sheer agony on the train for one hundred and twenty-five miles from Agra to New Delhi. Those were the most unpleasant hours of my life! The ticket agent assured me that I would be riding in first class, and I suppose I was. I could only imagine the horror of those poor people in third class accommodations.

Cramped into a small compartment with seven other people, I sat on a wooden bench uncomfortably bouncing along as the train wormed its way at a snail's pace to New Delhi. I felt as though I had been catapulted a hundred years into the past by a time machine.

The scenes that passed by the train window in review gave evidence of India's industrial adolescence. The most technologically and scientifically progressive nations on earth are comprised of people who at some time in history embraced the Christian faith. It may be an over-simplification to blame Hinduism for India's poverty but there is a definite corollation.

Finally, New Delhi—at least tolerable by Western standards—appeared and our train ground to a halt. The familiar odor one smells everywhere in India still pervaded the atmosphere. But here, thankfully, "sacred" cattle are restricted and kept from turning the thoroughfares into pastures.

In the cool of the evening I walked to a cafe for a bite to eat, surprised and pleased to find hamburgers on the menu. While I munched my supper I noticed a cluster of hippies gathered at one of the tables—three girls, three boys. I went over for a chat. Why, I asked, had they come to India? Their answer was no surprise.

"We've come to India to learn about Hinduism," their spokesman told me. All six had experienced the euphoria of LSD. All six considered the drug useful in opening the mind to the existence of the supernatural beyond everyday experience. All six admired the religions of the East, saying there was no distinction between the secular and the religious in the daily lives of the Indians.

My time finally ran out and I bade them goodbye, hurrying for a bus to the airport and a plane for Calcutta.

In the city where I had first landed, I continued my pursuit of information on Hinduism. I visited one of the temples which is a religion shrine in Calcutta. Professional beggars mobbed me the moment I stepped from the car. I could not give anything to a single beggar for fear of the consequences. Money for one meant money for all—or else!

Outside the temple a *babuti,* entirely naked and squatting on the ground, practiced his meditation. Smoke from burning incense rose to his nostrils as he sat there motionless. I was told that he had been there since sunrise and would sit without moving until sunset. Dozens of awe-struck Indian people stood around watching him in silence.

Nearby sat several other Hindu holy men. All had long, flowing hair, prayer beads around their necks, and sandals on their feet. Several of them had flowers painted on their bodies. Where had I seen such fashions before? In the hippie enclaves of America, of course.

The cultural inspiration for the hippie movement has not come from Haight Ashbury or Carnaby Street. It has come from India. Furthermore, it was obvious that each part of the stereotyped hippie regalia has a meaning rooted in Hinduism. Starting from the long hair (signifying holiness gained through mysticism) and on through the costume to the flowers (symbolic of India's non-violence) I saw the similarities with Hindu religious garb, courtesy of the hippies and the rock and roll musicians.

All these sights above were seen outside the temple wall. Inside the court I viewed thousands of Indians pushing and shoving each other in an effort to file through a narrow passagway. A Hindu priest approached me, smiling. He greeted me in excellent English. Seeing that I was an American he recognized an opportunity to pick up some money by offering his services as a guide.

"They're all trying to get a look at the idol of Shiva," he voluntecred. "It can be seen through an opening in the passageway. Follow me. I'll move them out of the way so you can see the idol."

The priest walked toward the passageway and yelled something in Hindi, the language of approximately forty per cent of all Indians. A pair of Sikhs appeared on the scene and pushed the people aside, allowing me a full view of the idol. I was appalled! My reactions went beyond my natural contempt for idols as I viewed that awful thing. Garlands of flowers hung about its neck and money lay at its feet—money which the priests would pick up later.

The idol was black and had several arms extending in different directions. I could not imagine why Indians would go to all that trouble just to get a fleeting glimpse of such an ugly piece of stone.

"Perhaps you would like to know more about Shiva?" the guide querried. He beckoned me to follow him.

We walked past a small shrine where several Hindus knelt praying to a phallic symbol of Shiva. Above our heads the branches of a dead tree extended. Hanging from those branches were rocks tied on with a piece of string. "What's this for?" I asked, pointing to one of the rocks.

"Shiva is the god of fertility," my guide answered. "Often women come her to pray for a child. After the child is born the mother returns to this spot to hang a rock on this barren tree as a symbol of thanksgiving to Shiva."

It was a ridiculous thing to do, but so were so many of the non-sensical characteristics of Hindu worship.

My priest kept up a running stream of commentary. "It is difficult to understand Hinduism apart from a knowledge of the worship of Shiva." he told me, as if reading questions in my mind. "As one of the three Hindu gods, Shiva is by far the most popular. He has been worshipped in India for five thousand years as the god of destruction and recreation. He also promotes pain, self-mutilation, starvation and solitary meditation. Some consider him to be passionate, violent, and even licentious."

The priest went on to tell me that this belief often led Shiva's followers to orgies of eating, drinking and illicit sexuality.

"One of the most popular images of Shiva," he said, "is as Nataraja, lord of the dance. Shiva is the god of rhythm and mysticism which seems to interest so many of you in America. There are many aspects to Shiva and this in itself symbolizes the Hindu spirit."

I could not have agreed more with my guide, but I'm not so sure why he found it a source of pride.

Suddenly a bell rang and a crowd began to gather in an open square in front of the temple.

"You are fortunate," the priest said, "to have an opportunity to observe a sacrifice to Shiva. Come with me."

We hurried into the crowd of pilgrims and walked along until we came to the middle of the square beside two U-shaped wooden stocks. I wondered about them until I heard the approach of several small goats. One of them was untied and held while yet another priest prayed over it and poured a vial of water from the Ganges on its body. The crowd became hushed as the goat's head was clamped in the U of the stock. A man grabbed the goat's feet and held them so that its body extended perpendicularly to the stock.

Out of the temple stepped an Indian carrying a three-foot-long sword. With skill born of much practice he raised the sword and with precise accuracy severed the goat's head. Blood began spurting everywhere while a priest took a "holy" vial and held it to the bloody neck to collect what blood he could and take it into the temple as an offering to Shiva.

I raised my camera to take a picture, but the angry look of the Hindus around me and the cautioning glance of my priest-guide persuaded me not to make such an unwise gesture.

Five times this gory heathen ritual was performed in the next ten minutes. Each time, blood was collected and taken into the temple. After the last goat had been sacrificed, a child of about three or four years walked over to the stocks and, grasping it by the ears, picked up the goat's head and clutched it to his chest. His parents dipped their hands into the blood and smeared it all over the child's body in a desperate attempt to please Shiva.

As I stood there staring at the blood-spattered pavement, I was nearly overcome by physical sickness but even more sickened spiritually before this vivid illustration of the degenerate, demonic essence of Hinduism.

Jimi Hendrix is the lead guitarist and singer for one of the top rock groups in America called the Jimi Hendrix Experience. He is also recognized by many as the most accomplished rock and roll guitarist in the world. On the album jacket of one of his albums, titled "Axis-Bold as Love," Jimi and his two musical companions are depicted as twenty-armed Hindu gods with exotic priestesses brandishing swords at their feet. There are several holy men depicted, including one who is half-man, half-elephant. The god on the cover looks identically like the pictures of Shiva that I saw at the Temple.

Hendrix's performances are so vulgar and obscene that sometimes even his own followers find him disgusting. His sex-exhibitionist style of stage antics are understandable, considering the religion he represents commercially. His adoring fans by the thousands are greatly influenced by his endorsement of Hinduism. Bob Dylan has also added his endorsement of Oriental mysticism and reincarnation. In his recent song "I Shall Be Released" he sings, "I see my life come shining from the West out to the East ..." If Jimi Hendrix, Bob Dylan and other rock and roll entertainers are allowed to continue with their present practices they will succeed in accomplishing in a few short years for Hinduism what Hindu missionaries have not been able to achieve in centuries—the exportation of Hinduism to Western society.

Imagine my relief when finally I arrived at the Calcutta International Airport. I sighed with deep relief. The past three weeks had been the most fascinating days of my life, yet I did not regret having to leave it all behind. There would be many other stops on my schedule before I would see the cities of my homeland but none would be more important in my itinerary than ancient Singapore.

From various sources I had learned of a Hindu penance and self-mutilation rite called *Thaipusam* which occurs in Singapore once every year. An outsider can observe this rite at only two places on earth—one is in Kuala Lumpur (M a l a y s i a) and the other in Singapore.

Before leaving home I had scheduled a city-wide crusade in the beautiful Conference Hall of Singapore. It would take place several days before the rite was to occur. Whenever I inquired about *Thaipusam* my friends insisted that it was so horrible that a verbal explanation would not suffice to describe it.

"You must see it firsthand," they told me.

I altered my plans somewhat to allow me to be in Singapore for the day of *Thaipusam*.

Finally it came, and I rose at six-thirty to be ready. With several missionaries I drove to the temple where the penance rites are performed. We arrived at eight.

Obviously, careful preparations had been made and preliminary activity was already setting the stage.

People by the thousands were milling about the temple courtyard. I pushed my way through to the middle of a large open area surrounding the temple. There I discovered a dozen Hindus enduring self-mutilation and torture to appease their god Shiva. Before the day was over, dozens more would go through similar rituals, with minor variations.

I wandered aimless for about an hour, looking at everything I could. Then I decided to concentrate on one Hindu man and watch the various stages in the entire torture process of *Thaipusam* from beginning to end.

He was twenty-two, an Indian boy who spoke reasonably good English. Before he set out on his three-hour ritual I had an opportunity to talk with him. His father had been very ill and was not expected to live, the young man told me. If the father lived, the boy had promised Shiva that he would go through the rite of *Thaipusam.* This was his second year. His vow had stipulated that he would endure the punishment for three consecutive years.

"What do you feel while you are being tortured?" I asked.

"Nothing," my Hindu friend replied. "When the priest prays over us our minds go into a state of daydreaming. We're aware that there are people about us, but we really don't know what's going on."

"After we are tortured and prepared, we will walk

three miles to the Tank Road Temple where another priest will remove the torturing devices. Then we will come back to ourselves and we won't know a thing that took place in between. Though our flesh will be pierced in more than a hundred places, we will not shed a drop of blood. Our god, Shiva, prevents our bleeding as a miracle sign of his power."

The Hindu seemed to be like any normal young man and spoke calmly and confidently.

"Aren't you just a little afraid?" I asked.

"Definitely not," he replied.

I knew, however, that if he were afraid he would never disgrace himself by admitting it.

"I have fasted for two days, and I have not touched a woman for two weeks," he told me. "My body is purified. Shiva will protect me."

One of his friends interrupted our conversation. The ritual was about to begin.

I thanked the young devotee for the opportunity of visiting with him and stepped back to watch. Normally, a foreigner would not be allowed such a close look, but I explained that I was writing a book and needed information so they let me climb inside a rope that held back the crowd.

My new friend stood erect and motionless before the priests and helpers. First, a large superstructure called a *kavadis* was placed on his shoulders. His *kavadis*, weighing nearly a hundred pounds, was made of wood. The balance of the weight was supported by four protrusions which were strapped to his body. The *kavadis* was adjusted so that it would remain upright as the boy walked.

Above his head the *kavadis* supported an idol of Shiva decorated with feathers and flowers. A hundred skewers—spear-like devices about three feet long which are extremely sharp—littered the floor. They looked like a straight pin magnified thousands of times.

Four flat strips of light metal, bent into the shape of a hemisphere, were attached to the *kavadis*. They extended out over the boy's body, two of them laterally and two longitudinally. Thus, two curved metal strips extended over his chest, back and over both sides of his body. These strips had spaced holes in them through which the one hundred skewers would be placed. Later they would be aligned so they could be pushed into the young man's body as if he were a pin cushion.

When the *kavadis* was finally ready, the priest walked up to the young man and chanted from the sacred Hindu texts. The priest next touched the forehead of the boy who was to be tortured. A glazed look came into the young Indian's eyes. He began breathing heavily and gnashed his teeth, convulsing until several men were needed to hold him steady. His eyes rolled in his head and a hideous look stole over his face. I turned to a Hindu standing beside me and asked what was happening.

"We believe that when the priest touches the forehead that the spirit of our god enters into us to give us strength for Thaipusam," came the reply.

No wonder they don't feel any pain, I thought. *Demon power somehow prevents them from feeling anything!*

Right before my eyes I saw a young friend succumb to the possession of a demon spirit. Before the day ended I would see many, many more.

Now that the demon had entered my subject, the torturing began. Quickly, several Indians took the skewers, placing them through the holes in the metal strips and pushing them into his body. The entire process took about an hour. By that time his back, chest and the area under his arms had been pierced a total of one hundred times. I was horrified, but this was only the beginning!

Large fishhooks were inserted into the skin of his legs. Fruit was tied to the hooks with a string. The weight of the fruit pulled the hooks into the flesh, creating enough agony of pain to send a normal person into hysteria. Two spiked shoes were brought to him. They were made of two pieces of wood shaped like a foot with dozens of nails hammered through, the sharp ends extending upward. They were clamped on his feet, a painful addition but almost nothing compared to what he had already been through.

Next, pins were placed in his arms and in his face. After all this, they were ready for the final part of the ritual.

During the torturing process, some Indian musicians had created the proper atmosphere for the occasion. A couple of them played minor jazz-like variations on an instrument resembling a large clarinet. It was called a drumbed. The drummer had kept up a steady, pulsating rock and roll rhythm. The wierd accompaniment was quite appropriate for the heathenistic sight I had observed.

Now, the tempo and volume of the music began to increase. The crowd became tense. I looked over my shoulder to the family of the young man enduring the suffering. Two of his sisters began to scream and weep. One of them fainted. I realized that the worst part of the torture must be ahead.

The chief priest approached the group of mistaken Hindus holding two knife-like spears about six inches long. He was chanting while another priest opened the boy's mouth and grabbed the end of his tongue, extending it from his mouth. Slowly the priest pierced the boy's tongue until the small spear was half-way through. Then, the priest left it in that position. It would be there until the boy had walked the three miles to Tank Road Temple.

The priest was not through yet. His assistant held the boy's mouth open wide while the priest took the second spear and pushed it into one cheek and through the boy's mouth until it pierced the other cheek. This spear also was left in the boy's mouth.

My emotions ranged from disgust to amazement to horror. I would not have believed a human being could endure such torturing if I had not seen it with my own eyes.

After three hours of this "preparation," the boy still stood there motionless. In this condition, with nails from his spiked shoes piercing his feet with every step, he would walk three miles before being relieved of his penance vow.

Slowly, very deliberately, he began his journey at what seemed to be the proverbial snail's pace. The expression on his face turned to a pleading, anguished look. Perhaps the presence of mind required to begin the walk had brought him out of his trance enough to awaken feelings of pain. Tears filled his eyes, but there was no way that he could cry out. Embarrassment was not the deterrent now. His tongue and mouth were rendered immovable by the spears that pierced them.

Tears came to my eyes too as I watched him walk away. Finally I buried my face in my hands and wept. *If only I could tell him of the love of Christ!* I thought, *If only he knew that all of his penance could accomplish nothing! That salvation is by the grace and mercy of Christ who himself suffered for our sins!*

I had seen enough for one day and turned to leave. On my way out of the courtyard I passed by a heavy wooden cart. Four ropes with large meat hooks were tied to the cart. One of the Hindus informed me that these hooks would be placed in the back of a man and he would pull the cart in that manner. The Indian insisted that if I would only stay a few more hours I could see it. But I could not bring myself to do it. I had had my fill of the awful penance rites.

I walked by a two-year-old boy whose tongue and cheeks were about to be pierced. Even an elderly woman was being tortured for Shiva. Age was no restriction.

Farther along I came upon some teenagers dancing to the same music that had been played during the penance rites. In my book, *Rock and Roll: The Devil's Diversion*, I had discussed the relationship between demons and rock and roll dancing. Now, I was to observe an apt illustration firsthand. Dozens of teens gyrated wildly, going through the same sensual gesticulations that I had observed in the dances of American teenagers. The rhythm of the music was the same pulsating and syncopated tempo used in rock and roll. What was happening here in Singapore could be observed in most teenage dances in America.

Suddenly a teenager screamed. His body became stiff and he fell to the ground, writhing and kicking. It took four men to hold him steady. Other teenagers who had been dancing began to suffer the same symptoms.

"What's happening?" I yelled to a man standing nearby.

"We dance to this kind of music until the spirit of our god enters into us," he answered.

I watched, somewhat frightened now, as one teenager after another screamed and was torn by convulsions under the influence of demon powers. The stimulus of the beat had been used as a medium to put them in a state of mind whereby demons could enter into them.

In America I had mentioned the connection between demons and dancing, but most people were skeptical. They considered my statements somewhat fanatical.

"Seeing *Thaipusam* would certainly erase their doubts," I murmured to myself.

Finally I reached the door of the courtyard. I took out my notebook and wrote: "This has been an unforgettable experience—seeing such an exhibition of raw demon forces in action."

I lifted my eyes to heaven, unable adequately to express in words the thanksgiving that welled in my heart. I was thankful for having been raised in America by Christian parents, thankful for the night I accepted the free gift of salvation through Christ, thankful for eternal life that is available through Him, thankful for the privilege of knowing and serving a God who requires only praise, not penance, from the people He came to save.

My long search came to a close. It had led me from the squalor of Calcutta to the thriving Eastern port of Singapore and from the Equator to the foothills of the Himalayas. In six weeks my senses had been assaulted by stimuli alien to my Western conditioning; my mind had boggled at strange phenomena. I had made as extensive a tour as possible of Asia and Southeast Asia. I had struggled to assimilate and interpret what I had seen and heard.

I had discovered the meaning of transcendental meditation and had distilled the essence of Hinduism. I felt qualified now to pinpoint the origin of the inspiration for the hippie movement and where it might be headed. I could now predict what might be in store for America if the present trends continue.

Having had experience in rock and roll, I considered myself able to interpret its meaning and that of its entertainers.

But most important of all, I had acquired through this long journey a greater appreciation of my relationship to Jesus Christ my Lord. O that more would know Him!

As the plane lifted off the runway at Singapore International Airport I once again took out my notebook. "My search has ended," I wrote.

I looked out the window. The mainland of the Malaysian peninsula faded farther and farther into the ocean of deep blue water. My vow to write a book on my experiences came again into my memory. I pondered the subject, and what the title might be. Three major, overwhelming topics recurred again and again in what I saw, dovetailing perfectly in an ominous pattern of prophetic gloom that cast its shadow over the world.

What else but *Hippies, Hindus and Rock and Roll.*

A Sequel

THE TRIUMPH OF WALTER

If one soul is worth more to God than the riches of the entire world, is any amount of time and money too much to spend in helping to bring one "home"?

On one leg of my globe-circling trip I boarded a plane in Bangkok for a flight to Saigon. During the flight I was describing on paper my experiences with the French hippies in Banaras during their *hashish* party. Suddenly I was startled to hear my seat partner speaking to me.

"I was looking over your shoulder and noticed what you're writing," the young American man said. "Have you been to Vientiane, Laos?"

"No," I replied. "What's there?"

"Plenty of hippies," the stranger replied.

"How do you know?" I asked.

"Because I'm one of them," he said.

"You're a hippie?"

"Don't let the clean clothes and short hair fool you," my new friend said. "You should have seen me yesterday. My hair was hanging down to my shoulders and my clothes were typical of those usually associated with hippies. I had sandals, prayer beads—the works! But I ditched them and got a haircut because I was afraid I might not make it through customs in that outfit.

He leaned closer. "The drug traffic in South Vietnam is tremendous ... I've got a pound of marijuana in my suitcase. I plan to make a big profit on it in Saigon."

I hadn't told the young man anything about myself. I hadn't even mentioned that I was a minister writing a book about hippies. But he continued to talk freely, volunteering information without any questions from me.

"I noticed by what you're writing that you've

watched *hashish* being smoked," he went on. "I've tried my share of drugs, I guess. My parents live in Southern California. I left them about a year ago. Since then I've traveled and smoked pot or taken LSD nearly every day. I've read what people say about marijuana, but I'll tell you the truth ... it may not be habit forming but it sure has messed up my mind! I used to have ambition ... know what I wanted out of life, you know? Now, I don't care about anything. Marijuana has completely taken away my will to live. All I care about anymore is getting high on drugs. It's getting so bad that I'm scared! I've freaked out so many times that I think I'm losing my mind ... I think I'm too far gone to turn back ..."

I sat in silence as he poured out his heart to me. I saw that God had brought this young man across the path of a believer in order to show him the Way. I prayed for a moment to tell this young man about the One who could bring purpose and meaning to his life.

"I've traveled around the world searching for something and I don't even know what it is that I'm looking for," he rambled on. His voice grew tender and serious. "There's got to be more to life than this. I've tried Hinduism and the hippie philosophy, but it's getting me nowhere. I don't know where to turn. I hadn't planned to fly to Saigon today, but at the last minute I came ... for some reason. My parents haven't heard from me in months. None of my friends or family know where I am. I'm frightened at what might happen if I don't find soon what I'm looking for."

"Young man," I said, "I hate to sound trite or to

over simplify the matter, but I know exactly what you're looking for. You are looking not for some*thing* to bring meaning to your life but for some*one*—and that Someone is Jesus Christ."

I went on to tell him all that Christ had done for me and what Christ could also do for him.

He listened intently to every word I said. When I finished he sat for a moment thinking.

"Sir," he said, "*this* is what I've looked all over the world for. But no one ever told me that. I'm going to throw away the marijuana that I have. My search ends right here. I'm going home to my parents!"

His statement shocked me. I hadn't even mentioned that he should return home, but this is the first thing he thought of.

By the time our conversation ended the plane was landing at Saigon. My friend had boarded the flight with another hippie friend still with his long hair and hippie garb. The friend had chosen to sit in the rear of the airplane even though there had been a vacant seat between me and my new friend.

"I'm sorry," I said, "but I didn't catch your name."

"Walter," he answered.

Just then his hippie friend came walking up the aisle. He stopped at Walter's seat. "C'mon, man," he said, "let's hit the streets and get the scene."

Walter looked at him, hesitated for a moment and then replied, "All right, but I'm only staying for a couple of days. I'm going home to my parents."

"Man!" the other said. "Who have you been talking

Walter replied, "I've just met a very wise man who told me what I've been looking for. This hippie life is not the answer. My search is over."

As we walked off the airplane, Walter looked for a place to get rid of the marijuana in his suitcase but he couldn't find any quick way to dump the drugs.

"I'll just have to try to sneak it through customs," he murmured.

I preceded him in line. The customs agent carefully looked through all of my belongings. I knew they would find Walter's marijuana if they searched his suitcase as diligently as they had scrutinized mine.

I watched as Walter walked up to the agent. The officer asked to see inside the suitcase, but when Walter reached into his pocket he couldn't find the key. He remembered that he had left the key to the suitcase in another pair of pants that was packed inside the suitcase.

"If you want to see inside I'll have to break it open," he told the customs officer.

The agent considered the possibility of breaking in, then changed his mind and motioned for Walter to go on through without being checked. He walked over to me.

"Someone is sure looking out for me," he whispered.

We parted at the airport because we had different destinations in Saigon. As Walter walked away with his hippie friend I was certain we would never meet again. I thanked God for that brief opportunity to tell him of Jesus Christ, but I was dubious about the total effect of our conversation.

Sure he said he would go home, I thought. *But he'll probably get involved with prostitutes and drugs here and forget everything I told him.*

Under the inspiration of the moment I conceded that Walter was willing to quit living as a hippie and shape up. But I anticipated that in a few days he would change his mind. I disliked being skeptical, but I had every reason to be.

Several days later I left Saigon one day earlier than planned, not knowing that the dreaded *TET* offensive was about to begin. I had objected strongly to this alteration of my schedule even though a ticket agent had insisted that I must do so to make the proper airline connections. But now in another part of Asia I read in the newspaper: "Viet Cong Overrun Saigon—Evacuation Orders Given." Fewer than twelve hours had passed from the time I left until the bombs and rockets began raining down destruction on the city in the Viet Cong's most destructive offensive of the war. I had barely gotten out on time, thanks to the providence of God.

Exactly two weeks from the last day I had talked with Walter I arrived in Hong Kong on a flight from Singapore. There is probably only one place in the Hong Kong International Airport where one might meet someone who had deplaned from another flight. I was at that spot when suddenly someone called out, "Bob Larson, what are you doing in Hong Kong?"

I turned and found myself staring at Walter the hippie.

"And what are *you* doing here?" I asked, happy to see him once more.

"Well, didn't I tell you I was going home?" he grinned.

Walter hadn't made it out of Saigon before the Viet Cong attack. Consequently he had been stranded in Saigon until it was safe for a plane to leave. "Today," he said, "was the first flight out and I got on board."

Walter and I stayed together for three days in Hong Kong as guests of missionary Paul Kauffman and his family. Walter had never been around Christians in his life, and God was providing in this way another opportunity for me to tell him about Christ and God's plan of salvation.

My search had ended. I was on my way home.

Walter's search had ended too. He also was on his way home. As we parted in Hong Kong he told me, "Normally I wouldn't have paid any attention to someone like you who talked about Christ and lived such a deeply religious life. But I can't seem to forget what you told me. We have been miraculously brought together twice. It seems that 'Someone up there' is directing my life. I just can't discount the unusual way in which we've gotten to know each other."

Several months after I returned to America I received a letter from Walter. He really had gone home. He wrote:

Dear Bob:

After you left Hong Kong I spent several days just relaxing and seeing the sights. I really enjoyed my visit there, and especially the hospitality shown to me by the Kauffmans. I had planned to leave about three days after you did, but lucky for me I delayed my flight an extra two days. Remember the plane from Hong Kong that crashed several days after you left? I had originally intended to be on that flight. I'm sure Someone is watching over me.

I've settled down and enrolled in college, taking courses in an airline pilot training program.

Sincerely,
Walter

I am not ashamed of the Gospel of Christ, for it is the power of God unto salvation ... to all who believe.

God's Plan of Salvation for Your Life

I. God's Love:
John 3:16—"For God so loved the world, that he gave his only begotten Son, that whosoever believeth in him should not perish, but have everlasting life." God loves you and wants to impart unto you His peace and joy.

II. Man's Sinful Nature:
Romans 3:23—"For all have sinned, and come short of the glory of God." There are few people who would insist they had never done anything wrong.

III. There's a Penalty for Sin:
Romans 6:23—"For the wages of sin is death; but the gift of God is eternal life through Jesus Christ our Lord." Spiritual death and eternal separation from God is the fate of those who reject God's love.

IV. Christ Died to Pay the Penalty for Sin:
Romans 5:8—"But God commendeth his love toward us, in that, while we were yet sinners, Christ died for us." Christ loves you as a sinner and has paid the price for your sin.

V. Salvation is a Free Gift from God:
Ephesians 2:8, 9—"For by grace are ye saved through faith; and that not of yourselves; it

is the gift of God: not of works, lest any man should boast." Salvation is available by believing in Christ and is a free gift that you cannot earn by your own merit.

VI. Christ is Ready to Enter Your Heart:
Revelation 3:20—"Behold, I stand at the door, and knock: if any man hear my voice and open the door, I will come in to him and will sup with him, and he with me." Christ stands at the door of your heart (your emotions, intellect, and will) and only awaits your invitation to come and dwell within your life.

VII. You Must Receive Him:
John 1:12—"But as many as received Him, to them gave he power to become the sons of God, even to them that believe on His name." When you choose to receive Christ, you become a child of God.

VIII.. God Promises to Hear Your Repenting Prayer:
Romans 10:13—"For whosoever shall call upon the name of the Lord shall be saved." You can be certain that Christ will forgive your sins if you ask him to.

IX. When You Receive Christ You Have Everlasting Life:
I John 5:12—"He that hath the Son hath life; and he that hath not the Son of God hat not life." You possess eternal life the moment that you believe on the name of Christ as the Son of God.

X. Prayer of Commitment to Christ:
Lord, I acknowledge that I am a sinner and need your forgiveness. I believe that You are the Son of God and that You died for my sins. At this moment I invite Christ into my heart as my personal Saviour. With God's help I will serve and obey Christ as the Lord of my life.

BOOKS BY BOB LARSON

ROCK AND ROLL: THE DEVIL'S DIVERSION

☆ Answers the question "What Is Rock and Roll?"

☆ Explains the phsychological, physiological, and sociological influence of rock and roll.

Price: $2.00

CURSED SHALT THOU BE IN THE CITIES

☆ A frank analysis of the social ills facing America

☆ The cause and cure of rioting clearly outlined

Price: $1.00

Special reductions available on large quantity orders and special rates also available to churches and book stores.

Order from: **BOB LARSON**
BOX 425
McCOOK, NEBRASKA 69001

Music Sheets Available of Original Compositions by Bob Larson (75¢ ea.)

- "Ivory Houses"
- "I've Got The Lord"
- "Matchless Beauty"
- "The Nails In His Hands"
- "I've Pressed Through"
- "Creation's Song"
- "Why He Should Care"

LONG-PLAY RECORD ALBUMS FEATURING
BOB LARSON

THE HUMOROUS GOSPEL SONGS OF BOB LARSON

SIDE ONE
VOCAL

1. I Won't Pack My Bags
2. Livin' Out of Victory
3. The Little Green Pill Song
4. Grumblin' Christians
5. Nothin' Can Hold Me

SIDE TWO
VOCAL

1. Heaven's Dictionary
2. Don't Say Amen
3. The Gum Chewin' Song
4. What A Better Place
   (This World Would Be)
5. Seven-Day Christians

Orchestrated background with the "Nashville Sound"—Available in Compatible Stereo (also plays on monural phonographs) .... **Price: $5.00**

I'VE GOT THE LORD

SIDE ONE
VOCAL

1. I've Got The Lord
2. It's Not The Same Place
3. Sittin' In The Pew
4. Why He Should Care
5. Matchless Beauty
6. I Know A Power

SIDE TWO
INSTRUMENTAL

1. Now I Belong To Jesus
2. Count Your Blessings
3. The Healer
4. The Lord Of Glory
5. For All My Sin
6. Will The Circle Be Unbroken

Full orchestration and choral background, available only in compatible stereo (also plays on monural phonographs) .... **Price: $5.00**

ONE STEP FROM GOD

SIDE ONE
VOCAL

1. One Step From God
2. Ivory Houses
3. The Nails In His Hands
4. Salvation Of The Soul
5. I Know Who Watches Over
   My Soul
6. I've Pressed Through

SIDE TWO
INSTRUMENTAL

1. I Know Who Holds Tomorrow
2. When They Ring Those
   Golden Bells
3. Great Is Thy Faithfulness
4. In The Garden
5. Jesus, Jesus, Jesus
6. Take My Hand Precious Lord

Orchestrated background, available in compatible stereo—(also plays on monural phonographs)
Price: $4.00

BOB LARSON SPEAKS OUT ON ROCK MUSIC

Recorded Live in a High School Assembly $5.00
Also Available on Tape—5 inch reel, 3¾ i.p.s. $5.00

Order from:
BOB LARSON • BOX 425 • McCOOK, NEBRASKA 69001

BOOKS AND ALBUMS BY BOB LARSON
ORDER FORM

Gospel Music Albums
1. THE HUMOROUS GOSPEL SONGS OF BOB LARSON (vocal)...............$5.00
2. I'VE GOT THE LORD (vocal and guitar instrumental)......................$5.00
3. ONE STEP FROM GOD (vocal and guitar instrumental)...................$4.00
*All the above albums are playable on both monural and stereo phonographs.

Talk Albums
4. BOB LARSON SPEAKS OUT ON ROCK MUSIC (LP Record)..................$5.00
5. BOB LARSON SPEAKS OUT ON ROCK MUSIC (Recording
   tape, 5 inch reel, 3 3/4 i.p.s.)...$5.00

Books
6. ROCK & ROLL: THE DEVIL'S DIVERSION $2.00
7. HIPPIES, HINDUS AND ROCK & ROLL $1.50
8. CURSED SHALT THOU BE IN THE CITIES $1.00

Please order by number below.

Gospel Music Albums

1.____copy(ies) @ $5.00 each $________
2.____copy(ies) @ $5.00 each $________
3.____copy(ies) @ $4.00 each $________

Talk Albums

4.____copy(ies) @ $5.00 each $________
5.____copy(ies) @ $5.00 each $________

Books

6.____copy(ies) @ $2.00 each $________
7.____copy(ies) @ $1.50 each $________
8.____copy(ies) @ $1.00 each $________

Subtotal $________

(Add 10% for postage
and handling)   + $________

TOTAL $________

Name________________________________

Address_____________________________

City_________________State________

Zip________________

Send cash, check, or
money order to:
**BOB LARSON
BOX 425
McCOOK, NEBRASKA
69001**

THE BOOK THAT EXPOSES THE TRUTH CONCERNING THE HIPPIES, THE BEATLES AND MAHARISHI MAHESH YOGI!

★ "Bob Larson, a former combo leader and composer, now pictures rock 'n' roll as an insidious obsession which threatens the moral fiber of this country."

Dallas Times Herald

★ "Bob Larson, guitar playing lecturer and author, believes that rock and roll music, with its heavy emphasis on drugs and its permissive attitude toward sex, is doing more than any other medium to undermine the values of youth."

The Detroit News

★ "Bob Larson points to civil disorders and the hippie movement as outgrowths of rock and roll music."

Alton Evening Telegraph

★ "I am delighted for young people like Bob Larson who have such a keen insight into and understanding of the problems of their own generation."

A College President

★ "Bob Larson's technique of getting students to look at themselves and evaluate today's moral codes is the one true way of improving society's problems."

A High School Superintendent

www.ingramcontent.com/pod-product-compliance
Lightning Source LLC
La Vergne TN
LVHW050616200726
843508LV00010B/1885